"THEY"

WILL DO

ANYTHING

To steal our digital identity and victimize our lives.

Identity Theft and Internet Fraud

Wayne L Staley

They Will Do Anything

Identity Theft and Internet Fraud

Wayne L Staley

GOLD RUSH
HOSTING SOLUTIONS

"Technological ingenuity is allowing experts to create amusement parks for hackers. This will not end well."

John Hrusovszky
Chief Operations Officer
Gold Rush Hosting
jayjay@gr-hs.com

Photography and graphics by Phase Four Graphics LLC

Wayne L Staley
Natalie Groshek Staley

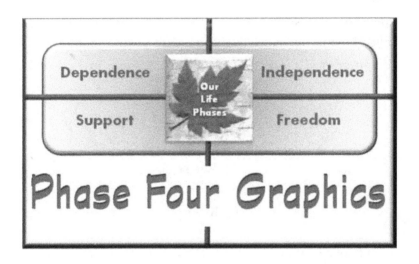

Copyright © 2016 by Affinity Systems LLC

ISBN-13: 978-1523480548
ISBN-10: 1523480548

Acknowledgements

The genesis for this book is the class "Internet Security and Identity Theft," developed for a senior audience. It is a prime example of private enterprise working with a governmental agency to protect our community. The following members contributed to the ongoing success of the program.

Tony Omernik

Norah Brown

Susan Osness

Pat Casey

Mike Theiss

John Prey

John Hrusovszky, Gold Dust Hosting Solutions, provided the succinct summation of the problem on page iii. Tony Omernik and Pat Casey suggested valuable inputs. Joe Groshek, Susan Groshek, and Amie Staley provided excellent examples.

Attempts at condensing the huge piles of subject content while retaining the necessary points was difficult. Natalie Groshek Staley worked to make the book as consistent, practical, and readable as possible. Her contribution was considerable and invaluable.

Thank-you, everyone.

Dedications

Military
Law enforcement
Fire fighters
EMT's
All those persons
working quietly behind
the scenes to prevent
fraud, keep our country
safe from international
attacks, and
find/punish Internet
criminals.

Table of Contents

"Identity theft (and identity fraud) refers to any crime where someone wrongfully obtains and uses another person's personal identifying information, typically for financial gain."

Source U.S. Department of Justice

1. The Dangerous New World of Identity Theft and Cybercrime

Nearly everyone has a story about identity theft. The most common involve stolen credit/debit cards, or hacked computers. Identity theft has evolved and multiplied into deadly dimensions. Using threats of dire consequences, cybercriminals/thieves coerce or manipulate individuals or groups into complying with their demands.

A bank employee related this true story.

A client received a call on her cell phone. When she answered, the perpetrator stated they were with the IRS. They said that when she filed her taxes, they contained errors incurring severe penalties, but the problem could be resolved by making an immediate payment.

She was told, "Go to the bank and purchase a Visa Gift Card, and then call back with the data needed to cash it." That data included the pin number, expiration date - everything needed to process it immediately.

The criminal used the cell phone GPS to track her location, and warned her not to tell anyone or contact the authorities. Extremely frightened, she complied with the demand. The thief was merciless, demanding that she purchase yet another card. She followed their instructions.

They coerced thousands of dollars from the victim. The greater price for her was going through a life-altering experience, showing her vulnerability and shattering her sense of security. It could happen to anyone.

In another example, the victim received a telephone call from someone pretending to be a grandchild involved in an emergency. He said his face was injured, and he could not speak clearly. The criminal called repeatedly, causing great emotional stress. The grandparents finally made contact with their grandchild, who was asleep at home, and did not hear his phone.

There are countless variations of the grandparent fraud.

An email from our web master provided a list of mobile devices that can be hacked, including the Android Smartphone. It was extensive.

Most of us are primarily interested in the personal dimension of cybersecurity and identification theft. We want to protect families, resources, and ourselves. Unfortunately, the problem grows geometrically with technology.

Someone, the Chinese government is a prime suspect, downloaded more than 21 million personnel records from the Federal National Personnel Office. The extraction included critical information on most, if not all, of our elected officials. Potentially, cybercriminals will use this data to coerce lawmakers into taking actions favorable to China, perhaps against our national interests.

This book explores the cause and consequences of cyberattacks and traditional data-acquisition methods. The societal implication of foreign governments acquiring personal data adds a formidable dimension.

While the primary focus is criminal activity, government/commercial data gathering is enormous and pervasive. Society is in the process of destroying moral boundaries once determined by religion. Data, like money, is fungible and impersonal, lacking character or ethics. In the digital universe, morality is nonexistent.

Knowing how to protect ourselves is critical. We must educate ourselves, and each other, to the real dangers posed by identity theft and cyberextortion. The consequences of ignorance are often dire, and permanent, putting citizens and society at risk. While unable to eliminate the danger, regardless of precautions, individuals can take steps to reduce the threat. Failure to take precautions increases the exposure to dangerous attacks.

Cybercrime is a complex problem, making it impossible to cover all of the problems and contingencies in this small book. Please consult the references used throughout the book and the bibliography.

Take immediate action when discovering compromised personal records, or when threatened with reprisals for refusing to comply with criminal demands. Start by calling your local law enforcement.

2. Information

Information is knowledge, and a tool for good or evil, depending on who and how it is used. Information resides at the power apex and can be used to plan and control situations and people.

Everyone must understand that information is driving the global disruption of all systems, and it is the new currency of personal and global exchange. To protect ourselves, we must accept this new reality and use it to our advantage. The more actionable data we have the greater the opportunity to turn situations to our purpose or profit, and protect ourselves from the actions of others.

Data, acquired from multiple sources, when merged with other data, become comprehensive information.

Personal data is our most valuable and sought-after possession. It directly links to wealth and power. Every citizen is in danger of financial damage and/or losing personal freedoms by the misappropriation and misapplication of their invisible data self.

Government, industry, and individuals spend billions of dollars searching for every type of information about us. Collectively, billions of dollars are spent protecting data, yet billions of dollars are lost to criminals.

Information is the competitive edge, enabling every type of human activity. This applies collectively, in personal relationships, health care, business competition, politics, and government.

Discussions on databases apply equally to legally and illegally acquired and stored data. These data are gathered, consolidated, bought, and sold. They all build personal profiles, and these profiles, lawful or not, have application in the real world. The difference is that businesses use the profiles to influence consumer behavior, governments for national security and social control, and criminals to steal.

Criminals use advanced technologies to commit age-old illegal activities, like blackmail, to target our valuables. They collect enough information to compromise people individually, socially, economically, or politically. If criminals chose to exploit that information, victims will comply or suffer the consequences.

Who are these criminals? The question is complex. Just as information is pervasive and complicated, so are those persons after our data selves.

3. Definitions

It is useful to establish a base of definitions. Security professionals address specifics in technical and precise terms, but for most of us, the focus is on understanding core definitions. These are identifying the criminals, understanding how they work, assessing the dangers, and taking the appropriate safety measures.

Personal Identifiable Information (PII or PID)

Personal Identifiers uniquely define an individual. The prime example is the most important, our Social Security Number. Other identifiers require expanded data elements, for example, a name, hometown, first pet, or passwords.

Examples of personal identifiers

- Passports
- Bank account numbers
- Credit /Debit Card account numbers
- Health benefit plan/medical identifiers
- Biometric identifiers - fingerprints, retinal scans
- Business identification number
- Internet protocols (URLs)
- Drivers license
- Military identification

Authentication/authorization systems

Modern information systems control access by using a two-step security process, authentication, and authorization.

1. Authentication systems require user names and passwords to access a site, for example, a bank account, health records, etc.

2. Authorization requires a PII to access the account. In theory, this step verifies the person seeking access is who they claim to be.

To the world of commerce, we are composed of PII's, user names, and passwords.

Cybercriminal

A cybercriminal (thief) is anyone who uses information (computer) technology to gain access to personal Identifiers. Given the data, they sell, combine, or use it to commit fraud. Increasingly, by using manipulative actions, that information can influence buyers and control behavior.

Profile of Hacker/Cybercriminal

Cybercriminals and governments, domestic and foreign, use sophisticated methods to steal vital intellectual property and identifiers from people, corporations, or government. They use this information to coerce or manipulate decision makers to take actions favoring those with the data.

In the early days of the Internet, hackers were often students and gamers that wanted to test their expertise. Today, identity thieves operate on every level of society and defy stereotyping. They range from playful hackers, family members copying carelessly managed data, to slick and successful hardened criminal gangs using the latest technologies.

The FBI reports that criminals once involved with drugs are finding this venue more profitable, and they ruthlessly operate like the mafia. They use on-line forums and other Internet tools to communicate, and are shifting to encryption systems to avoid detection.

The latest menace is cyberterrorism, where attacks on enterprises or infrastructure can disrupt service. This includes weapon systems, energy, and those national security systems most reliant on satellites and information technology.

Like every other vocation, cybercriminals have entered the age of specialization, using market segmentation and other sophisticated techniques. Some focus on health care, others on banking, etc.

The lesson learned is that cybercriminals use every tool available to legitimate business people, as well as the expanded tool set of illegal activities. Like roaches, criminals live everywhere.

Data

Data ranges from fragments to sets of facts that individually may be insignificant. Data is analog or digital, and may be alphanumeric or image. Data are calculated, correlated, analyzed, and distributed.

Metadata

Metadata is data describing data. Date and time stamps on photography are metadata, as are the type (format), image size, exposure time, and aperture opening. Another example is the time, location, caller, GPS location, and recipient of a cell/Smartphone call.

Database

A Database is a collection of data, an electronic file cabinet, organized, stored, indexed, and accessed using multiple types of algorithms and program languages. In theory, everyone contributes to a database, and everyone accesses it for information. The Internet is a prime example. Everyone using a computer adds to the total database, but not everyone has equal access. Few controls govern where information resides. Using the cloud, data exists in pieces on disparate computer systems.

Understanding information

Information is putting data into a useful form. Our home address, for example, is data, but when combined with city and state, it is a precise identifiable location.

Prior to the computer age, communications were slow. Even telephone and radio, while relatively fast, carried little digital volume or detail.

The information world today is pervasive, with a myriad of devices capturing and processing data of every type. Moore's law, regarding the speed and power of transistors, components of computer chips, predicts a doubling of power every two years. Bandwidth and Internet speed are the twin drivers of Internet capacity.

As computer and transmission speed and power increase, businesses and individuals have the ability to send or access ever-larger volumes of data/information to/from anywhere in the world. Global events unfold in real-time.

Identity theft definition

Identity theft occurs when someone acquires and uses personal identifiers to commit fraud. They acquire these data using a variety of methods, both on and offline.

Fraud

Cybercrime is about fraud, but this term has a pervasive nature and far-reaching consequences. Mail fraud and blackmail schemes often involve data obtained from the Internet.

a : <u>deceit</u>, <u>trickery</u>; *specifically* : intentional perversion of truth in order to induce another to part with something of value or to surrender a legal right

b : an act of deceiving or misrepresenting : <u>trick</u>

2a : a person who is not what he or she pretends to be : <u>impostor</u>; *also* : one who defrauds: <u>cheat</u>

b : one that is not what it seems or is represented to be

http://www.merriam-webster.com/

While the current emphasis is on Internet crime, the old fraud practices have exploded. The confidence, or con man, with new tools and opportunities, is even more dangerous.

Following is a list of the most common fraud schemes obtained from the FBI website at:

https://www.fbi.gov/scams-safety/fraud/Internet_fraud

Readers are encouraged to visit this comprehensive website. Read the advice for self-protection, and understand the correct actions to take if victimized.

Common Fraud Scams

- Telemarketing fraud
- Identity theft
- Advance fee schemes
- Health Care fraud/health insurance fraud
- Redemption/Straw man/Bond fraud

Investment-Related Scams

- Letter of Credit fraud
- Prime Bank Note fraud
- Ponzi schemes
- Pyramid schemes

Internet Scams

- Internet auction fraud
- Non-delivery of merchandise
- Credit Card fraud
- Investment fraud
- Business fraud
- Nigerian letter

Scams targeting Senior Citizens

- Cheap (but counterfeit) prescriptions drugs, anti-aging products
- Health care/Health insurance
- End of life issues: funeral arrangements and cemetery plots
- Telemarketers
- Reverse mortgage

To these add the following frauds

- Sweepstakes scam/Too good to be true
- Grandparent scam
- Stolen/counterfeit checks

- Home or auto repair scam
- IRS notifications
- Security scams
- Charitable donation scams
- Account alert scam

Search Engines, retailers, websites

Government, businesses, and criminals all capture data image in detail. On-line retailers, such as Amazon, have a database of our personal and financial information. If people can hack our account password, all they need is our credit card information.

Search engines, including Microsoft Edge, Google, Internet Explorer, BING, Yahoo, and WebCrawler, build on-line databases of Internet usage. Apple iPhone and iPad use Safari search engines, also capturing usage data.

Intelligent Personal Assistants (IPA)

The latest technological rage is Intelligent Electronic Personal Assistants. These programs interact with the user, learning personal habits, and executing vocal orders. They can remember passwords, control email, manage calendars, and give driving directions. They become "electronic" clones, and are capable of performing every transaction without the owner. These IPA's include Amazon Alexa, Facebook M, Google Now, Apple SIRI, and Microsoft Cortana. While wonderfully convenient and very trendy, they can be the ultimate Trojan horse.

Social Media

Social media has hundreds of sites, including Facebook, LinkedIn, Twitter, Instagram, and Flikr. Each of these contains enormous amounts of personal information on databases. The linkages expand greatly as users add friends. Worldwide, in 2016, there were more than 2 billion social-network users, as reported by WWW.statista.com/.

People post photos, which criminal's download to make fake ID cards, and potentially compromise retinal scanners. People also use Facebook to communicate trip plans, notifying friends of departure and return times. They inadvertently provide criminals with a window of opportunity.

As many times as people are told, "do not put anything on the Internet that you may regret," they continue to do it. Once posted, someone will copy and/or archive content even if later removed from social accounts.

Without going into details, selfies intended for personal or limited public use have destroyed careers. Among both pre-and teenagers, sexting is epidemic. It is also future ammunition tucked away for the right opportunity to coerce or blackmail a victim.

Poor social media practices are a setup for various types of ransom attacks, covered in Chapter 7, Types of Attacks, and subtitled, Ransomware.

Another example is Ashley Madison. The website, offering adultery opportunities, was hacked. They posted the "client list" of 37 million names and private information on the Internet.

Information put on the Internet can filter from the private to the public arena and it is forever. It can, has, and will be used against us. People may never know what opportunities were defaulted, or negative consequences incurred from a poor online decision.

4. Building our Digital Image and Personal Database

Health-care workers record the first personal identifiers, creating every persons information self by filling out the birth certificate. From the moment of that initial notation, the place, date and time of birth, data piles up geometrically throughout a human life cycle.

- Baptismal record
- Education records
- Athletic and scholastic awards
- News articles (hardcopy or online)
- Social security number
- Jobs-where, how long, function and performance
- Military records
- Marriage certificates
- Medical records
- Business affiliations
- Tax records
- Internet surfing practices
- Postings on social media
- Purchases
- Criminal activity, including speeding ticket
- Voting records
- Major purchases like homes, car, or property
- Financial data

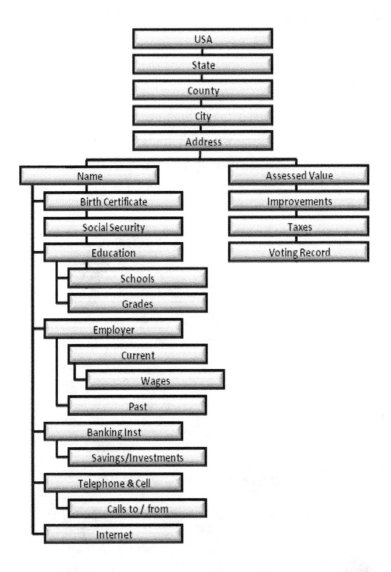

This database equates to our information image, or digital self. In the impersonal world today, this data self uses credit cards, buys homes, accesses ATM, and performs other financial transactions. Although a person may be physically at a bank, the digital self transacts the business. In the world of commerce, while a person and customer, we do not exist. To every computer in the world the digital self is real and we are not.

The problem is pervasive, and digital self-clones reside everywhere. Each time we apply for a new credit card, open an account at a store, buy a car, or go to a different medical facility, another data clone is born.

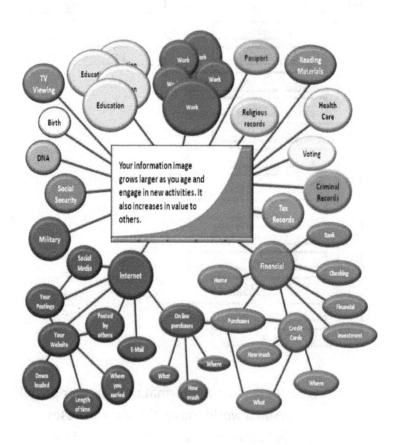

When we marry, the database doubles, along with the opportunity for criminal activity.

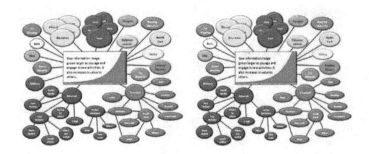

Every child increases the data pool.

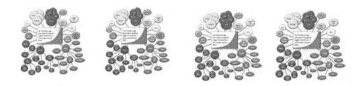

Nearly all types of stores, brick and mortar or on-line, record and digitize every transaction and movement. There are cameras in most business places, and on many streets. Devices are available to track cars, and to record every word uttered at work. People take photographs in virtually every environment, and given the size and stealth characteristics of recording equipment, targets will never know it.

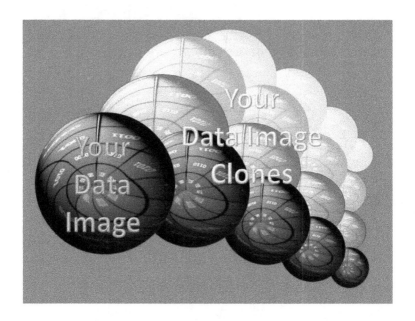

A mountain of accumulated data exists about each of us. These data are located in an unknown number of disparate databases, targeting us with commercial information, and political messages. In truth, everyone is subject to highly intrusive privacy violations.

Even if we live a pure and mundane existence, and are unconcerned about blackmail, in any form, the need to protect loved ones makes us vulnerable.

Mobile technology has moved the information reality from the office to the world, from voice to image and text, from status to content rich streaming flows. Actionable information is real-time and social media such as Facebook or LinkedIn enables global collaboration. It also makes cybercrime an international occupation.

These converging computer technologies provide the data to build information capable of knowing where we are and what we are buying, (cell phones, ATM, credit-card transactions), and sometimes where we are going (Facebook, trip planning on Google or MapQuest).

Even in our homes, there may be embedded technology in the telephone, computer, printer, television, automobile, lighting, heating/air conditioning, or any device capable of using computer chips. Collectively, these form the basis for the Internet of things (IoT).

Given all of these data-gathering technologies, identity theft is pervasive, and as technologies expand, so will the incidence of cybercrime. Unfortunately, this is only the beginning of the mischief possible as disparage databases are integrated.

Our digital self is brainless. Anyone who has access to it can/will use it to his or her advantage. It does not care- its only data.

That is why digital selves are vitally important. Jealously guard against every attempt to misappropriate your personal identifiers.

5. Identity Theft

Identity (ID) criminals act on the proliferation of data available from multiple sources, using it to buy product, on or off line, or getting cash from an ATM.

Per the following illustration, ID thieves are not looking for completed databases. They build their own by acquiring data in pieces and combining it to recreate a personal profile of our data image. This database does not have to be complete; only contain the appropriate PII needed to build a profile.

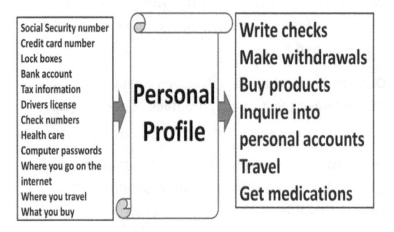

Criminals personally use the profile for illegal financial purposes, or sell it to consolidators, who in turn sell it to their customers. It is impossible to know the extent of these database chains.

Following is a summary of what ID theft involves.

Who you are, your data self

- Like it or not, to the commercial world we are the sum of our information.
- This information is more precious than anything else we own.
- Like anything precious, our information has value to anyone able to duplicate it
- Information is a commodity convertible into exchangeable products, from cash, to cars, or property

How they get email addresses

- Buy mailing lists
- Hack social media accounts
- Target specific demographics with phish, mail, or telephone calls

How they get data online

- On-line/Internet via personal email accounts
  - Hack computer (poor firewall)
  - Unprotected Wi-Fi
  - Phishing
  - Computer ID theft - planting virus, cookie, or code
- Smart Phones carry volumes of personal data but are poorly protected, making them a prime target for cybercriminals.

- Smishing is the same as phishing except using a Smartphone. The objective is to download a Trojan.
- Drive-by downloads.

How they get data offline

- Check reconciliation reports from bank
- Credit transactions
- At gas pump (last four digits of CC number)
- Blank (or filled out) checks
- Tax forms
- Military records
- Social media
- Trash
- Visiting our homes
- Telephone
- ID Card
- Mail (both incoming and outgoing)
- Modified credit card reader
- Copy / photo credit card information
- Cashier copies credit card data, SSN, name, address from checks, etc.
- Cordless phone signal intercepted
- Someone in our home finds info and sells it
- Lost or stolen wallet or purse

What they do with stolen information

- Impersonate the victim
- Spend as much money as possible in a short time
- Coerce the victim into taking actions against their will
- Sell it to other thieves

6. Cybercrime

Cybercrime takes many forms. Following is a list of the worst known invasions, compiled by David Goldman and Jose Pagliery @CNN Money. Please note the total population of the United States of America is roughly 320 million.

- US Office of Personnel Management - 21.5 million records compromised including most members of government and their security data.

- Sony Pictures suffered severe business interruption and threats when hacked by North Korea.

- Spamhaus is a spam-prevention service storing passwords for a fee. Hackers accessed 100,000 servers, involving an unspecified number of personal records.

- Heartland Credit Card was hacked for 130 million card numbers and other data.

- Target had 110 million customer accounts compromised.

- Anthem Insurance had tens of millions of records hacked and the information included all PII's plus medical histories.

- TJ Max had 94 million customer records hacked.

- Sony PlayStation suffered the data theft of 77 million credit card accounts.

- JP Morgan Chase lost information on 76 million customers and 7 million small business accounts.

- Experian Credit Service actually sold the data, for millions of customers, to a cybercriminal posing as an investigator. These data included Social Security Numbers, birthdays, work history, driver's license numbers, e-mail addresses, and banking information. The authors note that eventually, this may prove to be the most massive data breach in history. Cybercriminals downloaded this database 3.1 million times.

An analysis of this report yields many important lessons.

1. The combined total of compromised records is nearly double the total population of the United States. In all probability, the cybercriminals have our data images.

2. The people that are supposed to protect us, the government and credit card providers, fail to protect themselves, much less the citizens/consumers.

3. Some protection providers are unable to guard the data entrusted to them by customers. They make

money providing a service, but fail to deliver on the promise.

4. Credit Services, which all consumers are encouraged to monitor, are just as guilty of sloppy practices as their customers are.

5. The merchants who take our credit/debit cards are negligent by not using the latest technologies to protect us. Conversely, cybercriminals use every available technology to full advantage.

Consumers and citizens must take every step to protect our data selves. Until we take responsibility, and hold government, credit card providers and merchants accountable, the problem will continue to worsen. Even then, the criminals will find new, inventive ways to get our money.

7. Types of Attacks

There are numerous types of attacks, and each has a specific label with variations. This book covers only the basic ones. As users, or potential victims, preventative steps are similar.

Phishings

A Phish, pronounced "fish" is using email to obtain personal identifiers from computer users. It is a two-step process.

The first requirement is getting user's attention. Just as an angler casts lures into the water, criminals use email as bait. The email appears to be from legitimate sources offering goods or services. Other emails threaten service cutoff, or state improprieties of some type, such as income tax violations.

The emails may offer a variety of benefits, such as lower insurance rates, cheap loans, or free products. They may also contain threats to intimidate and manipulate users, with harsh consequences. Victims may receive a telephone call (vishing), or text message (smishing), asking for confirmation of personal information.

There are links to the criminal websites strategically placed throughout the email.

On the second step, the user clicks on a URL, linking to a spoof website that replicates a real one. Criminals ask users to provide the specific data that a legitimate website requires. Some websites look for many identifiers, other's lesser amounts for reasons discussed later.

When the user responds to the website request or the telephone call, the criminal collects another piece of personal identification at a minimum. Perhaps, in the case of banking information, criminals get enough PII to do immediate damage. Regardless, the computer user has now become a potential victim.

Every demographic is targeted.

Medicare coverage is a must-have for senior citizens and a major expense. Each year, senior citizens have the opportunity to make changes to their Medicare programs. They often lack the skills to recognize the clear and present online dangers, making them prime targets. A frequent phishing method is flooding seniors with Medicare-related emails.

- Timed for the period when seniors re-enroll in their current Part C and Part D programs.

- When they change from the current program to one that better fits their needs, or is available at a reduced rate.

The window for changing these plans lasts from mid-October through the end of the first week in December.

Criminals exploit these time constraints, by creating a false sense of urgently, getting seniors to act before looking at options, or doing their homework.

The following illustrations show emails I believe to be fraudulent. The first group are Medicare-related, but with a simple change to headings and content, could originate from anyone and be aimed at specific demographics. The software facilitating attacks is available on-line for a cheap price, making everyone subject to some type of phishing attack.

Look at the errors, and lack of professionalism. It is impossible to believe a financial, medical, or insurance company would allow the publication of such poor quality, non-professional documents.

These illustrations are available as a free download, under the title "They Will Do Anything - Identity Theft and Internet Fraud." www.competitiveamerica.us

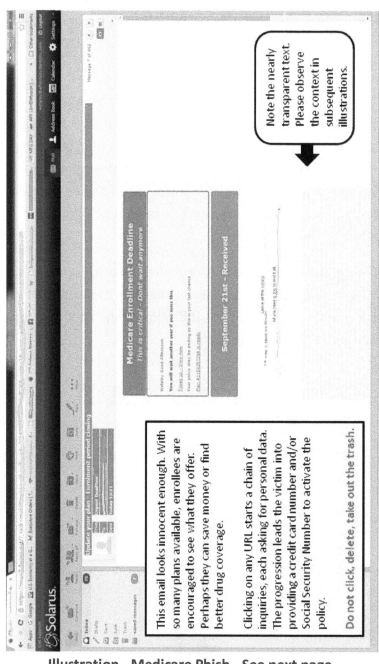

Illustration - Medicare Phish - See next page

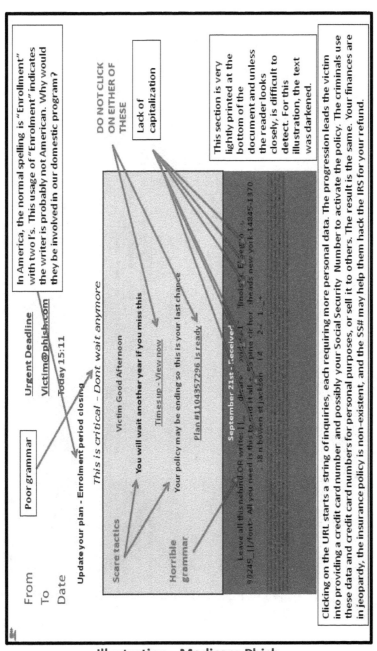

Illustration - Medicare Phish

The annotations in the illustration read:

In America, the normal spelling is "Enrollment" with two l's. This usage of "Enrolment" indicates the writer is probably not American. Why would they be involved in our domestic program?

DO NOT CLICK ON EITHER OF THESE

Lack of capitalization

This section is very lightly printed at the bottom of the document and unless the reader looks closely, is difficult to detect. For this illustration, the text was darkened.

From

To

Date

Poor grammar

Urgent Deadline

Victim@phish.com

Today 15:11

Update your plan - Enrolment period closing

This is critical - Dont wait anymore

Scare tactics

Victim Good Afternoon

You will wait another year if you miss this

Times up - View now

Horrible grammar

Your policy may be ending so this is your last chance

Plan #1104357296 is ready

September 21st - Received

Leave all this behind OR write | |_ dicare   xxt 2 +1   Ilnois x E' seg 0 . 90245_| |/font> All you need is this to end it all - SS pins cir hor sheads new york 14345-1370   18 n boxen st jackson 12   2 - 1 _+

Clicking on the URL starts a string of inquiries, each requiring more personal data. The progression leads the victim into providing a credit card number and possibly your Social Security Number to activate the policy. The criminals use these data and credit card numbers for personal purposes, or sell it to others. The result is the same. Your finances are in jeopardy, the insurance policy is non-existent, and the SS# may help them hack the IRS for your refund.

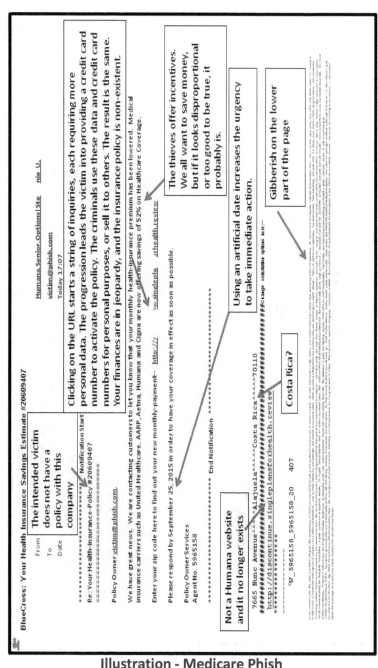

Illustration - Medicare Phish

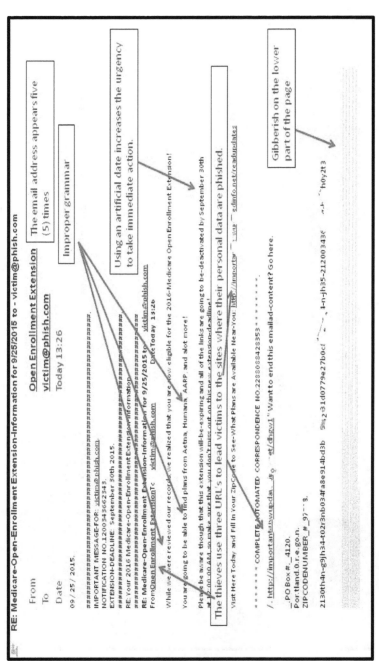

Illustration - Medicare Phish

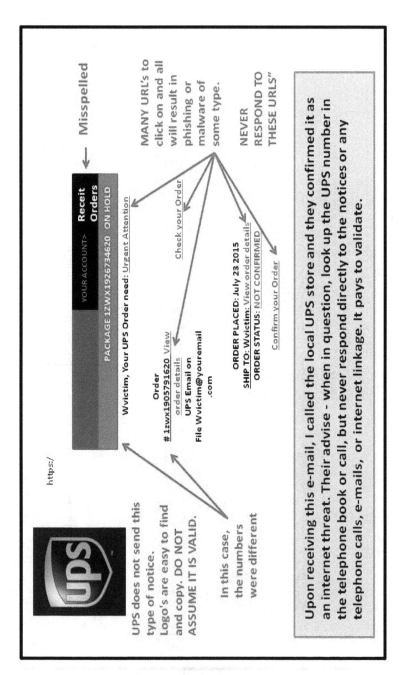

Illustration - UPS Phishing/Malware

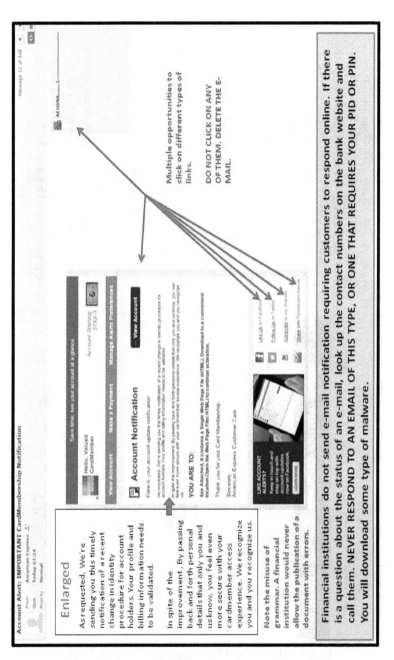

Illustration - Banking Phishing/Malware

Inuit Quickbooks (R) Online Accountant

QuickBooks ProAdvisor Security Alert

This is to inform you of important updates to the services associated with your QuickBooks ProAdvisor Program. We take security seriously and we want to keep you in the loop about important actions in your account. We detected suspicious or unusual activity on your QuickBooks Payment Account. As a result we have temporarily limited access to your account to ensure that you, and only those authorized by you. Have control over your account. We need you to verify your account information.

How do I verify my account?

Simply click here to log in and verify

We sincerely apologize for any inconvenience this may cause you, and thank you for all the ___.

Cyber criminals use this type of e-mail to subtly threaten people with a service cut-off, notification of an overdrawn account, or that service of some type has been stopped.

Similar notices state that monies have been deposited from an unknown source and verification is required to finish processing.

These phishing e-mails carry the full range of threats, from crooks acquiring PID's, to scammers planting malware or extortion software.

Assume the worst and delete these e-mails immediately. Remember, they remain on the computer until you take out the trash.

Illustration - Service Cutoff Phish/Malware

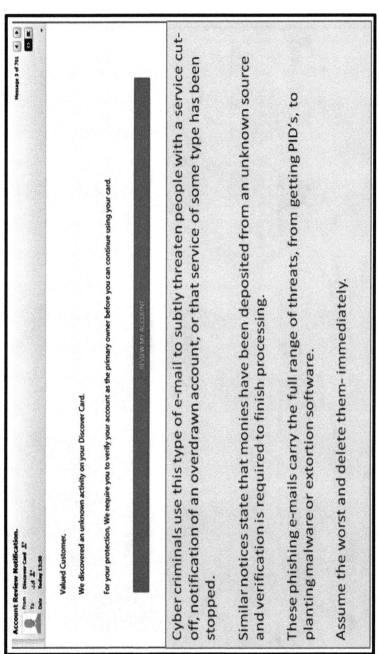

Account Review Notification.

From   Discover Card
To
Date   Today 13:38

Valued Customer,

We discovered an unknown activity on your Discover Card.

For your protection, We require you to verify your account as the primary owner before you can continue using your card.

REVIEW MY ACCOUNT

Cyber criminals use this type of e-mail to subtly threaten people with a service cut-off, notification of an overdrawn account, or that service of some type has been stopped.

Similar notices state that monies have been deposited from an unknown source and verification is required to finish processing.

These phishing e-mails carry the full range of threats, from getting PID's, to planting malware or extortion software.

Assume the worst and delete them- immediately.

Illustration - Service Cutoff Fraud

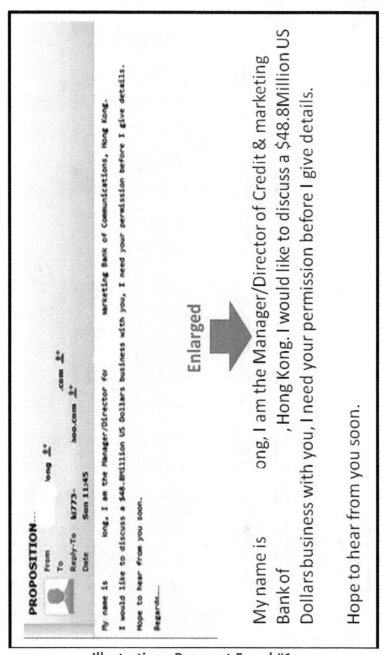

PROPOSITION....

From   long
To
Reply-To hi773-   hoo.com   .com
Date   Sun 11:45

My name is   long, I am the Manager/Director for   marketing Bank of Communications, Hong Kong.
I would like to discuss a $48.8Million US Dollars business with you, I need your permission before I give details.

Hope to hear from you soon.

Regards....

Enlarged

My name is   ong, I am the Manager/Director of Credit & marketing
Bank of   , Hong Kong. I would like to discuss a $48.8Million US
Dollars business with you, I need your permission before I give details.

Hope to hear from you soon.

Illustration - Payment Fraud #1

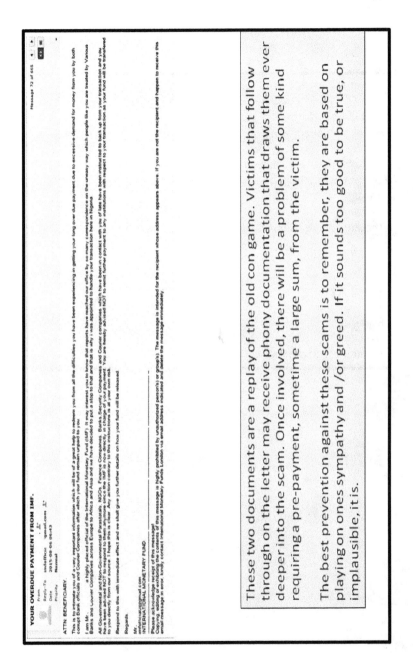

These two documents are a replay of the old con game. Victims that follow through on the letter may receive phony documentation that draws them ever deeper into the scam. Once involved, there will be a problem of some kind requiring a pre-payment, sometime a large sum, from the victim.

The best prevention against these scams is to remember, they are based on playing on ones sympathy and /or greed. If it sounds too good to be true, or implausible, it is.

Illustration - "Free" Money Fraud

41

Illustration - "Free" Money Fraud

Illustration - Banking- American Express

See corresponding notes on the next page.

43

1. Sloppy cropping of images downloaded from an Internet image.

2. There are a number of misspelled words. "Important Notice Regardig", "Your Account Number Begining" not beginning. Some words are capitalized, but this is a descriptive sentence, not a title.

3. This paragraph contains multiple grammar errors.

   - This is a fragmented sentence.
   - There is a comma where a period or semi-colon is required.
   - The next word, Kindly, is incorrectly capitalized following the comma. There is unusual word usage "we recognize you and you recognize us."

4. Four lines to click on, each one is a trap.

5. This line contains the words "Reclude a reccurence." No financial institution would use this phrase or publish this document.

6. "We look forward to serving you best" is an unusual phrase for a business document.

7. This paragraph states they are "sending the notice to everyone with an address on file with American Express," implying you are a customer. If you are not, where did the account number originate?

Criminals send the email to everyone. Some recipients will be cardholders, and they probably will not cross-reference their account numbers to their statements or credit cards.

8. This American Express logo on the upper right hand is another easy to use link, a pathway into the trap. Do not click on it.

Following is an email phishing attack with international origins.

From:	**Spammer Barrett <<u>negationrvf7@goznak-mpf.ru</u>>**
To:	
Subject:	**Account at risk**
Date:	Wed, 10 April 2013 16:40:16

```
ATTENTION

Your credit card account information is obtained illegally
from a merchant's records, credit card numbers are exposed,
putting those accounts at risk for fraudulent activity:
http://xwlyjotsov3jmd7wdk2m.fonsecaartes.com/language/ru-
RU/bigfoot.php?sub=online.citibankcom.8U9jLrBdRNO0PUos3rFA

Do not use public networks/computers to login to Citibank.
Do not ever disclose your banking information to anyone and
do not let anybody do internet banking on your behalf.
Copyright ¿ 2013 Citigroup Inc
```

Illustration - Banking Phish/Malware

Criminals use the identities obtained from phishing to rob bank accounts and buy goods/services in the victim's name. While some on-line offers are legitimate, ask if you can afford to gamble your savings and lifestyle to find out. It is important to learn the obvious signs of email fraud and stay vigilant.

This has been a small sampling; please visit websites where experts have meticulously documented different types.

http://lts.lehigh.edu/phishing/examples/social-networking

Banks and other financial organizations are covered in more detail later, but here are a few warnings.

- Financial institutions DO NOT send e-mails looking for personal information. Neither does the FBI, the IRS or any other governmental organization.

- NEVER click on a link in an email, especially from what appears to be a financial institution.

- NEVER provide personal or account information.

Pharming

The hacker plants a malicious code on the computer or hacks into a server, changing Internet protocol addresses. This automatically redirects users to a fake website or proxy server, where victims enter real data. This data may be PII only, but it is enough to let the hackers combine that data to get into other databases.

Pretexting

Assume the hacker obtained enough information from pharming. Using the personal data image, they pretend to be you, selling the information to other people who may use it to get credit in your name, steal assets or to investigate you.

Watering hole attack

An analogy serves the purpose to explain this method. All predators either stalk their prey or wait in ambush to attack. These criminals find a business website frequently used by authorized employees. They plan an exploit that takes advantage of system vulnerabilities or by using an employee code to gain access, and then plant a code on the site pages (the stalk).

When employees visit the infected pages, using the computer for legitimate commercial purposes, the compromised software allows the hacker to access the organization's databases, including the most private information (the attack).

Business organizations, like Target, are prey for watering hole attacks. The criminal potentially gets one of our digital clones, loaded with personal identifiers.

Ransomware/cyberextortion

Blackmail and ransom are timeless crimes, little changed throughout history. Criminals obtain something of value from us, and demand money, goods or services to give it back. The Internet has allowed criminals to perfect the techniques and take advantage of every change in technology. Cyberextortion has become a highly lucrative business channel for high-powered criminals.

A person's data represents opportunity to a criminal, while having greater value to the owner. The loss of access to data can cause panic and irrational response. Once the criminal has control of the computer, they blackmail the owner into paying for a decryption key to regain access.

There are different forms of this fraud.

One method employs pop-ups similar to the one below. Supposedly, the program "scans your computer," "finding" one or more non-existent virus infections. The program urges the user to download the software to fix and solve the problem, allowing the malware to encrypt the computer.

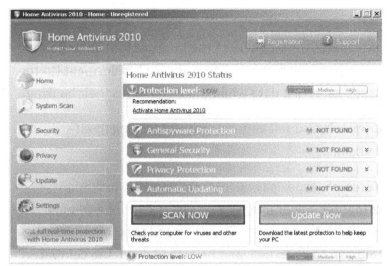

Illustration - Antivirus Malware - Source FBI Website

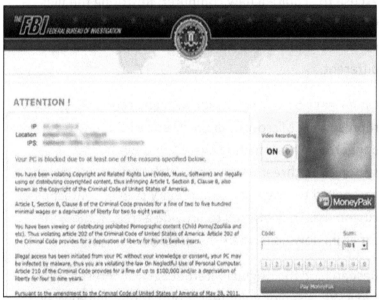

Illustration - New Internet Scam - Source FBI Website

Ransomware' Locks Computers, Demands Payment

Malware can be used in multiple ways. Locking up the computer, the criminal contacts the victim, asking for a cashier's check or Visa Gift Card. Optionally, the thief anticipates the victim uses the Internet for banking and other personal reasons. The malware lies dormant (to the user), gathering data while the victim does their banking.

Criminals also sell anti-ransom ware on legitimate websites.

Research, especially on Internet Security, makes a computer vulnerable, and on one occasion, a criminal hijacked mine. He called and wanted $500 immediately. I told him to go to hell, and he locked down the computer, destroying the boot system. The solution- it was a good excuse to acquire a new computer. Restoring the files from backups provided the opportunity to reorganize the contents. Without the backup, the ending would be different.

On another occasion, a caller with an accent, supposedly representing Microsoft, urgently stated there was a dangerous virus infecting every Windows operating system. The threat level was so high that Microsoft felt compelled to take the extraordinary step of contacting all customers. They offered to provide a free, immediate program download to fix the problem.

Researching the original Internet Security presentation for the RSVP, a senior volunteer group at the United Way, I followed the instructions given by the criminal up to the last point. Here is how it works.

The criminal emails the supposed fix, and it looks professional, absolutely like it came from Microsoft. This criminal was convincing and persistent, pleading to let him solve the problem. Criminals know every psychological ploy, and effectively use them all.

He sent me an email that instructed, "Click on the URL," downloading the solution, then "click on the update button."

Performing that last step would have loaded the malware, granting the criminal full control of the computer and its contents. When I refused, the crook passionately warned me of the severe consequences of my poor decision.

When dealing with criminals, the question is how much is your data worth to you, and have you backed up your files? If yes, there is an option to refuse, but depending on the type of attack, you may have to buy a new computer and rebuild the contents from backup files.

Paying the ransom may be throwing good money after bad. In the case of CryptoWall ransomware, Joseph Bonavolonta, Assistant Special Agent in Charge of the Cyber and Counterintelligence Program in the FBI's Boston office, stated:

> "The ransomware is that good... To be honest, we often advise people just to pay the ransom."

He followed up the statement with "You do get your access back"

Smartphone ransomware

The latest ransomware threat takes advantage of "private moments." People access a porn site, and are immediately infected with malware, which gives control of the Smartphone to the criminal. The device takes photographs or videos while in use for adult purposes. The criminal contacts the victim via telephone, email, or text message, threatening to publish these data and images if the victim fails to pay a ransom. Labeled "public shaming," this high growth industry has ominous implications. Unlike unlocking your data, the blackmailer can come back multiple times. The material may be released in spite of payment, or sold to other criminals.

Young adults, virtually all Smartphone users, constantly interact with social media, becoming prime targets for public shaming attacks.

Virtual kidnapping

The FBI issued an alert warning that virtual kidnappings are a growing criminal enterprise. While contact is primarily via telephone, the criminals use data collected through phishing and pharming to build a dossier on potential victims. Social media postings tell when people will be gone, and where they are going.

At the appropriate time, criminals contact family members, tell them the victim was kidnapped, and present the ransom demands. A variation is telling the victim, in a foreign country, they will be charged with a crime, such as drug possession, if they refuse to pay the ransom. In either case, it is difficult to know if the kidnapping is real or a swindle. Following is the recommendation from the FBI website.

> "If you think you are a victim, get to a place that feels safe, and then call someone who can help," said the crisis negotiator. "If you are a family member or loved one getting ransom calls, remember that you have more power than you think, because you have the money that the kidnappers want." He added that while some families think they can handle these situations alone, the FBI—which is the lead investigative agency when a U.S. citizen is taken hostage overseas—stands ready to offer its expertise and guidance to frightened families. "We can help," he said.

https://www.fbi.gov/news/stories/2014/november/virtual-kidnapping/virtual-kidnapping

A message to seniors

Your lifestyles, financial freedom, and peace of mind are under assault. You grew up in a time when trusting others was normal, and most people knew how to avoid frauds and cons. Those days are gone. While the Internet is a wonderful invention, it is a dangerous place. Internet criminals are MERCILESS. They will happily destroy everything you have worked for and come back for more.

Following is a warning and plea to family members.

When parents and grandparents are in jeopardy, it affects the entire family, by reducing future inheritance, and forcing once independent parents/grandparents to move in with family, or incur debts of other types. Show parents and grandparents what is safe and what is not.

A reminder to all

Even the young and sophisticated are victims. Internet predators do not ask for age before stealing identities and money. Complacency is just as dangerous as the lack of knowledge or experience.

Cybercriminals are experts at understanding every demographic. They know what you do, how, and when. They probe for every weak spot in personal or demographic behavior, just as they do senior citizens on Medicare.

There is a danger for everyone. Threats include business opportunities, student loans, music, on-line stores, and downloaded apps. These include travel, games, music, ringtones, and dating sites, and dozens of others. Do some research before downloading any apps.

8. Credit Card

Nearly everyone uses a credit or debit card, often many times a day. They are the plastic keys to our personal records and some of our wealth. While debit and credit cards are used in the same way, there are key differences. Debit cards are pre-paid, or take money from our banking account, while a credit card posts a charge on the line of credit extended by the issuer of the card. If a credit card is hacked, the card company normally removes the fraudulent charges, whereas money taken from a debit account is gone.

There are a number of important lessons learned about credit cards.

During a car trip to Alaska, on the first night in Canada, our location did not fit the credit card usage profile. The card supplier revoked it for security purposes. After several telephone calls, they authorized its use, but required a call with each use. We had sufficient cash to minimize calls, but still had a high telephone bill.

Several years ago, driving to California, we pulled into a busy gas station with only one empty pump. On the opposite pump, people were aimlessly wandering around a car. With personal warning gongs sounding, I checked for a scanner (a device that reads and steals credit card data) and filled up.

The following week the credit card company contacted us. Someone in Ft. worth, Texas was using the credit card to make multiple purchases from Wal-Mart. Each transaction was less than one hundred dollars, evidently Wal-Mart's threshold amount where personal identification is required.

We called the credit card company, using the telephone number on the back of the card, and provided specific card-usage data. After filing a disclaimer, the credit card company removed the charges.

Given its importance, when was the last time you really looked at your card?

The Anatomy of a Credit Card

The following illustration is a tool for understanding this important financial device. It was cobbled together based on actual images. I chose to combine the traditional American credit card with the newer technology used throughout the rest of the world.

Preparing the illustration demonstrated how easy duplicating an old style card can be. Given the permanent information embedded in the magnetic stripe, and a plastic embossing device, cloning the cards is uncomplicated. Entering "how to make a plastic credit card" into GOOGLE returned 25,500,000 URLS.

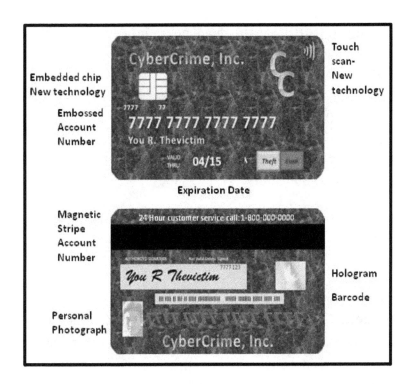

Credit and debit cards are the traditional instruments for identity theft and fraud. The card technology in the United States is dated and the security ineffective. For those reasons, credit-card companies and business enterprises are transitioning to the EMV chip technology long employed by most of the world.

EMV stands for EuroPay, MasterCard, and Visa, the developers of the technology (labeled "embedded chip New Technology") in the illustration. This includes scanning the "chip" (the RFID tag) and entering the PIN (Personal Identification Number), as done with a Debit card.

October 15, 2015 was the deadline for implementing this technology, but many merchants still have not installed the new system.

Look at your credit card and compare it to the example. Is the credit card company employing the latest technologies? If not, they are more worried about their profits than your safety.

Consumers must be aware that criminals use numerous methods to get the credit card information, but these new cards offer an incremental level of protection.

Cybercriminals use scanners and other electronic methods to capture data from credit/debit cards. The criminals have already learned to exploit the new card, remotely scanning the touch scan. Labeled "contactless identity theft," it demonstrates how criminals use the latest technology.

Ask suppliers/retailers if they are using the EMV technology to protect their customer's credit cards.

While failure to use new technology is a problem, the greater danger occurs each time someone handles your card. It only takes a few seconds to photograph the card using a Smartphone, and instantly send the information anywhere. Just as easily, criminals can write down the key identifiers or dictate them into a recording device. With the credit card number, pin number, name, and expiration date, they are a "digital you", and can use it just as you would.

- The lesson learned is to treat all credit cards as the key to our digital selves.

- Limiting the number of credit cards you own limits the number of clones associated with each one.

- Carrying too many credit cards is a special liability.

- Reduce the frequency of credit card exposure to criminals by using real money. While carrying large sums of cash exposes a person to other types of loss, pay cash for low-cost transactions. Anticipate higher expenditures and take enough cash.

9. Checks

Checking accounts are now old school, but for some applications, are safer than credit cards. Many businesses actually prefer a check or cash because they avoid the processing fee and enjoy immediate compensation. Others refuse to accept them under any circumstance.

While in California, we attempted to cash a check using a credit card and drivers license for verification, they refused to contact our bank. It was a moment of realization. Our digital image, used in an electronic form (ATM), had greater value than the human self did.

Checks create a whole set of problems. Fortunately, the solutions for most are relatively simple, but require changing some habits.

Modifying checks is easy. The only issue is how to steal them. Not surprising, one of the easiest and most prevalent methods is also the oldest.

It is called the mailbox scam, and here is how it works.

Written checks, in envelopes, are deposited in the mailbox, and the flag is raised. Before the carrier picks up the mail, a thief spots the flag, steals the letters from the box, and lowers the flag.

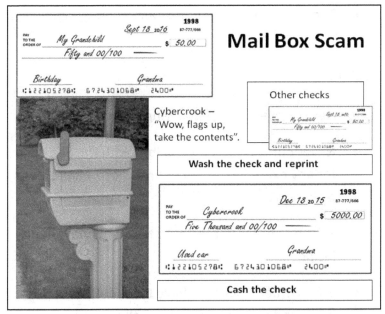

The criminal washes the written ink from the check, normally with a mixture of acetone, and lets it dry. They write the check to someone they have identification for, fill in the new amount, and forge the signature, often using a mechanical tracer. They cash the check or pay someone to do it.

There are documented cases where the criminal has used a sticky substance to remove materials from locked postal boxes. In other cases, they moved and/or destroyed the box to get at the contents.

The victim finds out when:

- The checks clear.

- The creditors fail to be paid.

- They are overdrawn at the bank.

Solutions

- Never leave a checkbook lying around.

- Never put checks in the mailbox with the flag up for any extended period of time, and definitely not over-night.

- Take payments to the Post Office, and mail them inside.

- When ordering checks, have them delivered to the bank, and pick them up personally.

- Always fill out checks by using a Uni-ball 207 Retractable Fraud Prevention Gel Pen. This ink integrates with the fibers in the check and is difficult to wash out.

10. Putting it together

Direct mail/marketing

Direct mail, viewed as a nuisance, is a conglomeration of the good and bad. Many mailings represent legitimate organizations, such as charities and political solicitations. Unfortunately, criminals find it a gold mine for personal identifiers and a lot more.

Even legitimate organizations collect data that finds its way onto mailing lists, databases, and eventually into the hands of criminals.

As seen in this photograph, mail marketers use every psychological and physical ploy available to manipulate a person's emotions.

Some mass marketers enclose money to "encourage" opening and responding to the contents. Coins destroy shredders, and force the recipient to open the mailing. Variations of this are gifts, often objects people are emotionally attached to, such as religious items, or too good to throw away. Some mailings contain checks, with the plea to return it along with a generous donation.

The following illustration is a typical component for a direct marketing document.

1	**Will you make a contribution today to help fund our effort?** ☐ Yes, I've enclosed my maximum contribution in the amount of: ☐ $15 ☐ $25 ☐ $50 ☐ $100 ☐ $250 ☐ $500 ☐ $1,000 ☐ My best gift: $_____

Please write your donation to (the charity, political group, etc.)

SIGN HERE TO VALIDATE YOUR SURVEY

2 X_____

I prefer to use my Credit Card - options:

3 Please charge my gift of $_____to my: ☐ VISA ☐ Master Card

4 Name on Card (please print) _____
Card # _____

5 Authorized signature _____
My email address is _____

1. It requests a donation of incrementally higher amounts. Normally, contributors write a check and put it in the return envelope, often to a PO Box number. The sender or marketing company receives and processes the check.

2. In this example, a survey preceded the request, and the sender is asking the donor to validate the survey by signing on the line.

3. The objective is to get the contribution by credit card on line.

4. The donor supplies an address.

5. The donor supplies an email.

The principle foundation or charity normally receives the money from the marketing firm, not directly from the donor. In this example, the donor has supplied critical personal identifiers to an unknown marketing firm.

- Name and address

- Email address

- Credit card number or checking account information

- The answers to the survey become information for marketing segmentation and future targeting.

Given these data, what are some potential consequences?

- The donor has created another digital clone and perhaps added to multiple databases.

- The marketing firm may be a criminal activity. If so, thieves can write checks, or wash the check the donor sent, and with the clean signature provided on the submitted surveys, forge the name, using a mechanical tracer.

- By using a credit card, the donor provides the criminal immediate access to their money.

- The criminal may sell all of the data to one or more criminals.

- In any event, the marketing company will sell the data collected numerous times to willing buyers, legitimate or illegal.

- Assume the marketing firm is legitimate, they still may be hacked and your private data stolen.

Here are three rules to make sure your money goes to a point of use instead of to the marketing firm.

- Give locally to your church, the Salvation Army, United Way, Warming Center, Food Kitchen, St. Vincent De Paul, etc. Local donations get a larger share of the money to those in need.

- Carefully research any charity by going to http://www.charitynavigator.org/

- Research any political action group and validate its legitimacy.

IRS Income Tax Fraud

Criminals obtaining personal identifiers from online, mailboxes, homes, hacking tax preparation services, and other sources, use these data to commit income tax fraud. The IRS reported that criminals had hacked 334,000 accounts, and the amount of lost information is unknown.

Using hacked user names and passwords, criminals accessed the IRS system, primarily the Get Transcript System, obtaining tax information on taxpayers. Changing the address, they filed returns sent to a phony address. The IRS discontinued The Get Transcript System.

Criminals find out the PII, including the Social Security Number, and file the taxes ahead of the victim. The check is sent to an alternate address. The refund may be a debit card. The victim finds out about the fraud when they legitimately file their taxes.

 One solution is to file as early as possible. You can also contact the IRS and set up a secondary password.

https://www.irs.gov/Individuals/Electronic-Filing-PIN-Requestsecondary password.

Health care

Our local medical facility recently posted this message.

"Our medical center" has been informed of a telephone scam in which people are receiving calls that are incorrectly identified by caller ID as originating from our facility. The caller offers medical bill forgiveness in exchange for credit card information. This is a scam. If you receive such a call, <u>do NOT</u> provide your credit card information. Instead, please contact your local law enforcement agency to report the issue. Thank you."

11. Your identity has been hacked

Following are clues that your identity has been hacked and criminals are using it.

- The credit card company calls and asks if you are making charges at the Wal-Mart in Ft. Worth, Texas, but you are in California.

- Someone applies for a credit card using your personal identifiers and the credit card company sends it to an address of their choice. Criminals use the card to make numerous charges. (It may be weeks/ months before you know).

- There are unexplained withdrawals from checking/savings/ATM accounts.

- The credit card company contacts you for payment or information.

- You find out when turned down for a loan or job.

- Stolen checks are cashed and cleared.

- A creditor sends you a reminder for a bill you already paid by check.

- You file a tax return but never get a response, or are told your taxes have already been filed and a refund check issued.

- Bills or other types of mail fail to arrive on a normal schedule.

- Calls arrive from debt collectors (they are not legally allowed to harass you. Get the facts).

  "The Federal Trade Commission (FTC), the nation's consumer protection agency, enforces the Fair Debt Collection Practices Act (FDCPA), which prohibits debt collectors from using abusive, unfair, or deceptive practices to collect from you".

  https://www.consumer.ftc.gov/articles/0149-debt-collection

- There are unfamiliar accounts or charges on credit reports.

- Credit applications are denied.

- Bills for goods/services not used or purchased appear on the credit card statement.

- The computer no longer responds and you get a ransom call.

Why be Concerned

- Stolen identity can cause lasting damage to your personal finances, credit, reputation, and ability to find employment.

- When a fraudulent loan, issued in your name, ends up in default, it damages not only credit records, but you may face potential liabilities. The results of a bad credit report

- Jobs - Employers check credit on applicants.

- The victim is unable to obtain credit, loans, or rentals.

- If a criminal using our ID is arrested, then jumps bail, an arrest warrant may be issued in the victim's name.

Take Immediate Action if Hacked or the Victim of Cybercrime

If you have reason to believe you are a victim of identity theft, cybercrime, take action immediately to maintain some control over the situation.

- Notify financial institutions and credit-card companies immediately. Change as many variables as possible. Cancel old credit cards and request new ones. Change every password. Put an additional layer of passwords on your financial accounts. Even if your financial institutions are not directly involved, it is impossible to know the extent of the fraudulent activity. Provide as much detail as possible.

- If you have a tax accountant or service, and/or attorney, contact them immediately. You may not need them, but make sure they are informed.

- Contact the toll free numbers of the credit card reporting companies. Place a fraud alert on your file. Carefully review all reports for fraudulent or questionable activity. The Arizona State Government provides the following contacts:

   Equifax
   www.equifax.com
   P.O. Box 740256 Atlanta,
   GA 30374 888.766.0008

   Experian
   www.experian.com
   P.O. Box 9532 Allen, TX 75013
   888.EXPERIAN (397.3742)

   TransUnion
   www.transunion.com
   P.O. Box 6790 Fullerton, CA 92834
   800.680.7289

- Close all suspicious accounts, and use the opportunity to review the need to retain those seldom used or obtained to get a discount.

- File a report with the local police where you think the theft occurred. Obtain and retain a copy of the report. Some frauds occur in demographics, such as the elderly, and law enforcement may prevent predatory actions on other citizens.

- File a complaint with the Federal Trade Commission (www.ftc. gov) by calling 877.438.4338 (ID Theft Hotline).

- Notify the FBI at https://www.fbi.gov/report-threats-and-crime.

- Refuse victimization. If faced with threats/coercion, notify the local authorities. If a victim undergoing a crime, get help discretely if necessary, or call 911. When contacting the authorities, use a different telephone. The criminal may be tracking the one in use, recording data, or both.

- Forcing you to get money, in any form, from a bank, ATM, or other financial sources is grand theft larceny, whether done with a gun or cell phone. Overcome any negative social attitudes about law enforcement. They are dedicated to helping you, and trained to deal with these situations.

Stolen wallet

A friend recently had her wallet stolen. She acted promptly, taking all of the right actions. Some of these steps duplicate the internet crime list.

1. Call the bank or credit card issuer; put a hold on all credit/debit cards.

2. Change all passwords for automatic payments and notify the bank.

3. File a police report. Go to the local/state website and download the correct procedure. Provide:

   - Credit/Debit card numbers
   - Check numbers/account numbers
   - Keep hardcopies and emails of all correspondence

4. Find your Social Security Card, hopefully in a safe place, and never in your wallet. The Department of Motor Vehicles will require it.

5. Got to the DMV and get a new license.

6. Change your email and every password for all bank accounts and on-line or brick and mortar retailer or service, such as Amazon.

Our friend was fortunate; the authorities caught the crook, in great part because she took all of the right actions, and supplied accurate information.

12. Recovery

Before discussing recovery from cybercrime or fraud, the victim must quantify the size of the problem and put it in perspective. At best, the entire process may prove difficult, and will take time to fix. Each case may have variables unique to the victim, but there are common actions everyone needs to take.

The following issues play a significant role towards recovering from a fraud attack.

- How long it took before learning about the stolen identity, and initiating action. Checking credit scores and all credit-card transactions are important to the fast discovery of fraud.

- The response speed of notifying all the concerned parties is critical.

- The level of professional support available.

- The hacker or criminal who has your digital image can now do nearly anything you can do. Whatever precautions you have previously taken to prevent or limit additional fraudulent activity will prove important.

- The type of theft that occurred, such as, lost or stolen wallet or purse, computer virus, family

75

member using victim's personal information, credit card, etc.

- Whether or not the criminal used the personal information or sold it to other criminals, creating additional layers of opportunity for fraud and headaches for the victim.

- The level and thoroughness of key records are an immediate issue. Financial institutions and law enforcement will need detail information to deal with the fraud.

- What the victim's credit report and creditworthiness were before the exploit?

- Personal relationships with the various institutions are important. They may also know the real you as well as the digital image. Talk to them.

- Major credit-card companies have fraud squads, and details help them trace and find the perpetrator. Apprehending the criminals plays an important role in limiting future exposure and speeds the recovery process.

Recovering from identity theft and avoiding liability for the debts that criminals create is a long and arduous journey and may tax the patience and resources of victims for years.

- Phone calls

- Written correspondence

- Keeping track of creditors

- Responding to letters

Working with credit bureaus, law enforcement agencies, credit-card companies, creditors, etc., take time and patience. Paying attention to detail will be important for each step.

For most victims, the incident will pass, but some monetary loss may occur. For those threatened by financial insecurity or destruction, the recovery process will be difficult and often requires professional help of various types.

13. How to Protect Your Identity- Summary

General rules

- If it looks too good to be true, it is.

- Know where you stand on your finances. Check your bank and credit card statements against your records. This is first line of defense to discovering possible fraud. If something does not seem right, ask questions. Increase the level of attention to details including methods for paying bills. Examine your habits to find contributing factors.

- When contacted by someone claiming to be your credit card supplier, promise you will call back. Use the telephone number on the back of the credit or debit card. Never respond to an email. Call the card company.

- Check credit reports regularly. Obtain free credit reports at www.annualcreditreport.com.

- Carefully check all of the medical information you are given. Is it correct? If not, return to the health care provider and get it corrected.

- Before you take out another credit card, remember, you are also creating another digital clone. While in the process, discontinue all unnecessary or unused credit cards.

- As counter-intuitive as it sounds, pay cash.

- Insist that merchants use the latest technologies. As the customer, exercise the power of purchasing.

Staying safe on line

- If you do not know precisely where clicking on a URL is taking you, DO NOT CLICK.

- NEVER click on an email link from what appears to be a financial institution or the IRS.

- Extend the thought to include Facebook and other social media.

- Do not give out personal or financial information online unless you have initiated the contact and know whom you are working with.

- Use strong passwords and keep them secure.

- Use unique passwords for each site.

- Do not save passwords on sites. They are not encrypted and are fair game.

- Password protect your WI-FI.

- NEVER provide personal or account information, especially a social security number, or financial data of any type to any site you do not absolutely trust and that lacks a lock symbol.

- When purchasing products online, make sure there is a "lock" icon on the status bar of the Internet browser. It means that the site is secure and information can be safely transmitted.

- Pay attention to the URL line. Shortened, special characters or URLs that do not match the website are common tricks. Do not click on them.

- When on Facebook or other social media, do not click on any pop-ups.

- Free content is not free. Criminals infect products like music, videos, movies, and free apps with viruses, and/or malware.

- Surfing adult sites invites a malicious attack.

- If you receive a request for information or verification from a company you do business with, do not click on a link in the email. Type the name of the website into the address bar to check if the URL relates to the sender.

- Hover the cursor over URLs and see if they take you to the appropriate location.

- Use a good virus protection program with a Firewall.

- Exercise caution on social networks because links can lead to malicious downloads.

- Use high security settings.

Search results

- Cybercriminals have a variety of tools. They download viruses, worms, Trojans, Adware, or code to redirect the computer, or hold it hostage. Here we are at the mercy of online habits and anti-virus/protection programs. No browser or search engine will prevent a cyberattack.

Disposing of used equipment

- Before you dispose of a computer, phone, or other mobile device, get rid of all the personal information stored on it. This is not simple. Even erasing the drives does not eliminate the data, it just resets the index, and new data is written over the old. Software is available that destroys these data, but anyone can purchase software capable of recovering lost files.

- The safe way to dispose of a computer is to remove the hard drive and drill holes through the memory plates. There are disposal/recycling services that reliably destroy the hard drive, but do your homework before selecting one.

Staying Secure Offline

- Keep financial information and records in a safe place, preferably locked up. Safe deposit boxes are a great place to store important paperwork.

- Limit what you carry to required identification and necessary credit/debit cards.

- Collect incoming mail promptly.

- When ordering new checks, ask to pick them up instead of having them mailed.

- Know the individuals you are working with.

- Take all outgoing mail, especially those with checks, to the post office or a collection box.

- Never leave mail in your box overnight, especially those with checks.

- Do not leave valuable information in places where others can easily find it, including your checkbook. This applies in your home.

- Shred all documents containing PII when you no longer need them. These include:

  - Receipts
  - Credit offers/ Preapproved card offers
  - Credit applications
  - Insurance forms
  - Medical statements
  - Medication container labels
  - Checks/check copies
  - Bank statements
  - Expired credit/debit cards
  - Investment statements

Vacation checklist

- Call and provide your itinerary to the credit card company.

- Provide for snow removal or lawn care.

- Put mail on vacation hold, even for short periods.

- Put newspapers on hold when gone or have a trusted neighbor pick them up.

- Do not broadcast trips, for example on Facebook. Tell the stories when safely back at home.

14. The Commercial World

This chapter deals with a data world known almost exclusively to information specialists. In this world, everything about us accumulates in databases. "Everyone" uses these databases to target what we do, when we do it, and they attempt to program our actions and response.

If this sounds analogous to George Orwell's book "1984," there is a reason. The ability to control people by access to personal information is a clear and present danger. It exists now, not in some future scenario.

Every business records transaction data in detail, using scanning technology, smart phones, portable devices, calculation methodologies, and even pen/pencil and data entry. These transactions include orders, inventory movement, labor reporting, shipping data, warehouse transactions, receiving documents, reporting every business action in some form. In addition, they record and control all communications, frequently as e-mails, telephone calls (metadata) and cell/Smartphone calls.

The consumer world is increasingly moving to the Internet. Business-to-customer (B2C) and business-to-business (B2B) applications are escalating.

Every transaction on the Internet leaves a traceable footprint back to the buyer. These include product purchase, ship-to location, credit card information, shipping notification, tracking, and delivery receipts. These collected financial footprints include purchase orders, names, bank codes, etc., as both real data and metadata.

Collectively, these create a condition labeled "big data." The prior evolutions of technology left business and government searching for viable analytical data. The problem today is how to manage and convert large volumes of data into useful information products.

Big data requires massive storage capacity and access from anywhere in the world. It is not realistic to carry a computer with enough storage to conduct business and personal affairs. As individuals, we have big data problems as real to our situations as they are to business and governmental organizations. We also want access to every database for our own use. The cloud serves the purpose.

Enterprises of every type are working on integration and automation. One example is Customer Relationship Management (CRM).

CRM is a tool of Internet retailers, capturing real and metadata from customer inquiries/purchases. The system tracks specifics - what customers/suppliers buy/sell/want or do not want, e-mail addresses, demographics, communications, event monitoring, project management, and collaboration programs.

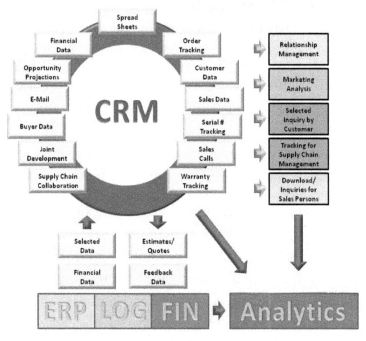

The information in a CRM system provides an accessible, real-time database useful for mining information, and provides event alerts and analytical summarization. CRM data models predict and influence buying behavior. Practitioners call the systems "the voice of the customer." Every major retailer and many manufacturing enterprises utilize this technology.

One could argue about the intrusion of CRM into personal privacy, but it manages and analyzes large volumes of detailed information. Mining for strategic, tactical, and individual purposes, facilitated by structured data, makes information accessible globally in real time. This includes information about us. The point is, where there is a means to acquire information, there is a way to process it.

15. The Cloud

Cloud computing, a misnomer but a useful term, defines storage and processing solutions.

Gartner defines cloud computing as

> "A style of computing in which scalable and elastic IT-enabled capabilities are delivered as a service using Internet technologies."

Cloud service providers have massive or shared computer power and storage, paid for by subscription or amount of service used. These include multi-tenant service bureaus and web based processing, such as Software as a Service (SaaS), Service Oriented Architecture (SOA), and Application Service Provider (ASP), fall under the cloud umbrella.

The cloud provides a great way for knowledgeable computer users to backup their files. This step dramatically reduces the vulnerability to hijackers.

16. Health Care

The Affordable Care Act (ACA) created a de facto national health care database. Electronic Medical Records form the core quality standard in the ACA, and establish the base for compensation. The problem is that a greater population of recorded factors increases statistical errors.

Every person receiving medical care has those services and conditions recorded in broad and extensive detail. These records play a significant role in the quality of health care.

What medical record keeping means to you

The major concern dealing with information is data accuracy. The old acronym, GIGO, or garbage in, garbage out, has frightening implications for patient care.

There are steps every consumer must take to protect themselves.

Review, in detail, the medical records you receive. Make sure the listed procedures were performed and outcomes properly reported. Check the accuracy of all prescriptions. Contact the medical service provider to correct any errors.

When finished with old records, shred them. Do not leave them lying around where others can steal or copy them. Never throw them in the garbage where dumpster divers can find and steal personal information.

17. Integrated Data Bases

The integration of our health care records into the IRS database is part of the Affordable Care Act, fulfilling the true objective of the legislation. Potentially they form the

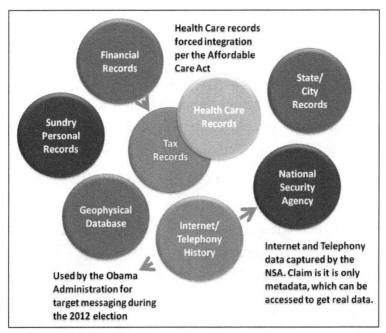

National Database of you and me. These data are useful to manipulate or coerce us into taking action against our free will, or for the greater good as defined for an idealistic objective with which we may not agree.

18. International Threats

China hacks into every American system, stealing industrial and governmental information. Industry and consumers alike are targets. The accumulative effect is millions of personal records hacked with immeasurable consequences.

Unfortunately, the attacks have taken a turn to the dark side. In 2009, the Chinese government attacked Google, Yahoo and other Internet companies. The Chinese government gathered data on their human rights leaders, and appropriated intellectual property.

The North Koreans hacked Sony Entertainment, who produced a comedy titled "The Interview," plotting an assassination attempt against Kim Jong-un, their supreme leader. From all appearances, the North Korean government failed to find the film humorous.

What this means to readers

Coercion at a personal level is the new and the most insidious form of international cybercrime.

Readers need to view this as a dark omen for the future. When the National database is complete, everyone can be controlled and manipulated through coercion, reward, and punishment if/when-governmental agencies exploit our information.

19. How Information is used to control behavior

Government and business use information for a variety of commercial and private purposes, for and against citizens/consumers. For this paper, there are two major areas of concern. First is information security. The second is the overall threat for business, government, and the media to control and manipulate information to sell or coerce us to a point of view.

The media can/does cooperate with government to deliver precise political messages. These situations can quickly evolve into "propaganda" and "programming" to control behavior.

The following chart breaks information use into four categories, starting with knowledge, and progressing into social control. Somewhere between propaganda and control, the free press disappears, compromising all personal liberties and rights. The process can be so subtle; society in general may not realize it has occurred until it is an accomplished fact.

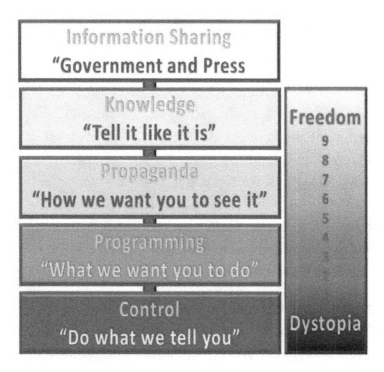

Knowledge "as it is"

This category represents a free press dedicated to finding and reporting the truth. A neutral press will fight government attempts to block, control, or manipulate information. Individuals are able to manage personal data.

Propaganda "How we want you to see it"

The second category involves the opportunistic manipulation of or denial of facts by the government to the press and media. A complicit media moves propaganda closer to a state of social programming. Business/governments use personal data collected from a variety of sources for targeting.

Programming "What we want you to do"

The third category represents where the press and the citizenry start to lose control. Access to information is limited in terms of what, how, when, and where. The result is controlled content, used to reinforce bias, or program opinions to conform to political correctness. Privacy no longer exists.

Control "Do what we tell you"

The last category represents a loss of liberties. Government manages information to coerce, intimidate, or otherwise control the populace. Medical care becomes a control mechanism, and cronyism prevails. Free enterprise is dead. This is a dystopia.

What we can do

We are at one of those points in history where the operative word is "control." There are steps we can take to guard against propaganda, programming, and coercion.

1. Be aware when people use information to control, coerce, or blackmail you into giving them something of value. If they do, contact the authorities or an attorney. If people are pressuring you, they may also be doing it to others.

2. People gather information in small chunks. It is important to question the validity of data, both

on and offline. Work past the headlines and dig into the issues. Find out the real facts.

3. People have a bias, and consume information reinforcing those opinions. Try to expand the input base and question the source for accuracy.

4. We rely on expert and group opinion. These sources may be wrong, or manipulated into a course of action.

5. Be constantly on guard when told to do something for the "greater good." Who established what it means and why it should it drive our actions.

All of this sounds ominous and frightening, but it is the reality of our society. Paying attention to details and questioning strange or abnormal situations is smart.

Make fact-based decisions. Getting complete information and making good decisions is the greatest defense against identity theft and Internet fraud.

Criminals strike without mercy. Take precautions to avoid an attack, but if it happens, fight back using every legitimate means possible.

Easy Rules

1. If it looks too good to be true, it is.

2. Unless you know exactly what or who it is:

   Do not click.
   Delete.
   Take out the trash.

Bibliography

Carson, Patrick Michael,. *10 Rules For Safer Web Surfing!*

Chabinsky, Steven R., Deputy Asst Director, Cyber Division, Federal Bureau of Investigation, GovSec/FOSE Conference
FBI SPEECH
Chank, Andrea,. Lien, Tracey,.*Outages at NYSE, United Airlines, WSJ.com expose digital vulnerabilities*
Chickowski,Ericka,.*10 Shocking New Facts About Ransomware*

Conn, Joseph,. *CLA Health breach puts data at risk for 4.5M*

Coty, Stephen,.*The Lasting Impact of the Ashley Madison Breach*

DIGICERT,. *Don't get Caught by Phishing scams*

Experian,. *Recovery Tips for Identity Theft Victim*

Federal Trade Commission   consumer.ftc.gov D,.Fair Debt Collection Practices Act 15 U.S.C. §§ 1692-1692p,. *Debt Collection*
Federal Trade Commission consumer.ftc.gov May 2015,. *Debt Collection*

Geller,Damon,. *Banks Quickly Abolishing Your Ability to Use & Store Cash*

Gerstner, Lisa,. *How to Fend Off ID Thieves*

Gores,Paul,.*Thieves using data-skimming devices to steal debit card info*

Heller, Michael,. *OPM hackers stole 21.5 million records, 1.1 million fingerprints*
http://www.scambusters.org/veteranscams.html

Https://security.intuit.com/**phishing**.html,.*Scams: Phishing, Smishing and Vishing*
https://www.fbi.gov/news/speeches/the-cyber-threat-whos-doing-what-to-whom
https://www.google.com/?gws_rd=ssl#q=National+Check+Fraud+Center

https://www.irs.gov/Individuals/Get-An-Identity-Protection-PIN

Keith,. *FBI Alert as Virtual Kidnap Scams Rise*

Kenny, Gavin,. *I Know Everything About You! The Rise of the Intelligent Personal Assistant*
Liptak, Kevin,.Schleifer, Theodore, Sciutto, Jim,. *China might be building vast database of federal worker info, experts say*

McGee, Oliver, PhD,. *Tech expert discusses cyberattacks' far-reaching consequences*

Morris, Cassandra,. *14 Identity Theft Methods Used by Criminals*

Nakashima, Ellen,. *Chinese hack of federal personnel files included security-clearance*

National Check Fraud Center,. *Check Washing What is it?*

Navetta, David,. Ross, Susan,. *The EMV Liability Shift is Coming (What Merchants Need to Know)*

Pagliery, Jose ,. *Ex NSA Director China has hacked Every Major Corporation in The USA*

Perez, Evan,. *Anthem probe looking at China as possible source of hack*

Pumper, Michael,. *Internet of Things Security 4 Problems and Solutions*

Ranger, Steve,. *The New Art of Way; How trolls, hackers and spies are writing the rules of conflict*

Rashid, Fahmida Y., *Black Markets for Cybercrime a Specialized and Mature Economy: Report*

Riley, Charles,. *Hackers threaten to release names from adultery website*

Rosencrance, Linda,. *How to Spot (and Stop) ATM Skimmers*

Rowley, Kris,. *Cybercrime and How it Affects You*

Sanger, David E., Perlroth, Nicole,. Shear, Michael D., *Attack Gave Chinese Hackers Privileged Access to U.S. Systems*

Savage, Marcia,. *ACH fraud scams total $100 million, FBI says*

Schaefer, Sara,. *IRS scam named worst of 2015*

Shinder, Deb,. *10 ways to avoid being the victim of identity theft*

Symantic,. *Fraud Alert: Phishing — The Latest Tactics and Potential Business Impacts – Phishing White Paper*

Tamarov, Maxim,. *Fobber: Drive-by financial malware returns with new tricks*

Tommie Singleton - AICPA,. *The Top Five Cybercrimes*

VanAntwerp, Tom,. *How Hackers Breached the IRS and Stole $50 Million*

Weise , Elizabeth,. *IRS hacked, 100,000 tax accounts breached*

Weise, Elizabeth Weise, USATODAY,. *IRS hack far larger than first thought*

Wells Fargo,. *Common Fraud Methods*

Wells Fargo,. *Wells Fargo Survey: Many Small Businesses Not Ready for EMV Chip Cards*

www.wisconsinsmp.org,. *12 Tips to Protect Yourself from Health Care Fraud*

Zorabedian,. https://nakedsecurity.sophos.com/2015/10/28/did-the-fbi-really-say-pay-up-for-ransomware-heres-what-to-do/

About the Author

Wayne Staley established Affinity Systems LLC, a system consulting company, in 1997.

 Educated in computer technology, business, and manufacturing systems, Wayne managed Corporate Information Technology, Materials, and Logistics, for multi-plant, vertically integrated metal processing and forest products manufacturing corporations. His experience includes Manager of Shop Operations for a complex fabrication facility.

Certified in TQM, NAFTA, and Project Management, Wayne audited Mexican operations, worked on integrated supply chain programs with Chinese suppliers, and collaboration programs with Dow Chemical, developing processes and new products. He performed numerous studies on energy, products, and doing business in Mexico. He served for eleven years on the City/County information processing commission.

He has managed numerous projects, including business strategy, Enterprise Resource Planning (ERP), and Lean (VMP) in manufacturing, government, distribution, and convention management.

He created Phase Four Graphics LLC, a graphic arts company, phasefourgraphics.com, and CompetitiveAmerica.us, advocating for American industry. Phase Four Graphics LLC developed training materials for ERP, Supply-Chain Management, Strategy, and Process Improvement. Wayne is a member of the Society Manufacturing Engineering, and a past member of APICS and AITP. He has presented at meetings, conferences, and seminars, for all three. He has authored seven books.

Decision Making in a Disruptive Reordering

Technology has changed our world forever, but the disruption has only begun.

Automation is changing the workplace, and human jobs are being replaced by machines. These changes also disrupt the education system.

Entrepreneurship represents the path to success for many people. This requires recognizing and taking advantage of opportunities.

The common denominator for success in a disruptive world is developing good decision-making skills.

ERP Lessons Learned-Structured Process

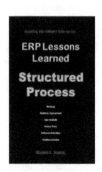

ERP projects are tough work but very important for the future of your company. Competitive pressures will only intensify, and companies will compete at ever-faster speeds.

Those serving as project team members, directly or on functional teams, hold the operational effectiveness of your employer in your hands. As you take actions to get the job done, the outcome will affect many lives.

ERP Structured Process, forged in the heat of project management, is not an intellectual exercise, but a systematic guide to executing a successful project. It starts with understanding operations, and ends with successful operational systems.

ERP Information at the Speed of Reality

Every type of business must execute effectively and move from a physical and information reality of weeks and days to minutes and seconds. The smart enterprise builds intelligence gathering in near real time, taking full advantage of faster operations.

ERP projects are complex, involving strategies, internal assessments, evaluation of multiple alternatives, and making critical business decisions. They require assigning high performers to project teams, taking them away from important daily activities. ERP systems are so expensive that failure is not an option. Evidence based decisions and a structured process lead to successful results.

Pathway to Adaptability

The marketplace demands correct products, appropriately priced and available now. Speed is King!

Enterprises must become very smart, building real-time intelligence into every activity. Without accurate information foundations, and process improvement, adaptability is not achievable and significant opportunities will be lost.

"This book has invaluable information on LEAN Six Sigma Methodology that is used in my company, and has been used as a reference point in many of our LEAN Focus Groups across the country. I highly recommend Wayne Staley's book." Amazon review by Black Belt.

Freedom and Opportunity-Stop Redistributing and Downsizing America

The current greatest barriers to growth are the policies of the Federal government, quickly followed by the forgotten or unlearned lessons of history. We are all part of the problem, and building a viable America demands positive actions. If we fail to rekindle the American dream, it is our fault - yours and mine and every citizen of America.

Coupled with Canada by geography, demographics, and economy, North America can become the opportunity capital of the world. It will take positive leadership, courage, and a government that enables entrepreneurs and business instead of imposing penalties, redistributing wealth and power, and downsizing America.

Productivity Prescriptions for Health Care

The primary mission of health care professionals, executive leadership, and associates is delivering quality health care to patients.
Productivity Prescriptions for Health Care provides a structured program methodology for defining and implementing contemporary process improvement programs specifically designed for the special requirements of health care organizations.

Productivity improvement programs are required for future Health care sustainability, with quality and efficiency the twins for success.

www.ingramcontent.com/pod-product-compliance
Lightning Source LLC
Chambersburg PA
CBHW071225050326

40689CB00011B/2458